MilkRice 2

Stories for Children

Published by Popsicle Books, 2013

an imprint of the Perera Hussein Publishing House

ISBN: 978-955-0041-04-6

First edition

Printed and bound by Thomson Press

To offset the environmental pollution caused by printing books, the Perera Hussein Publishing House grows trees in Puttalam – Sri Lanka's semi-arid zone.

MilkRice 2

Compiled and Edited by
Ameena Hussein

Popsicle Books
COLOMBO

For Hana, when she is ready

CONTENTS

city

A BEAR NAMED BOO

Afdhel Aziz

This is the story of a bear named Boo. Boo was a friendly bear, who lived for two things: eating hakuru and playing cricket.

He lived with his friends, Mr Perera and Patiya. Mr Perera was a gecko who ran the local library and Patiya, a mongoose, played in a papare band (trumpet, in case you were wondering).

The three of them lived in an old blue house, surrounded by a garden filled with araliya trees.

One day, Patiya and Mr Perera decided to surprise Boo with a birthday present. They knew how much he loved nature and trees, so they took him to the Enchanted Forest which was famous for its Magic Trees, so tall that they seemed to almost reach the sky.

They walked into the Forest and soon found that they were very, very lost. Everything looked the same and they felt like they were going around in circles. Finally, they stumbled into a clearing and paused for a minute to catch their breath.

At this point, a policeman was walking by and saw all of them panting in the clearing. He was a chameleon, with a skin that changed colour as he talked.

"What's going on here then?" he demanded, affixing Boo with a menacing eye. "You're not supposed to be here. This is a restricted part of the Enchanted Forest!"

"We're very sorry, sir," said Boo earnestly. "It's just that we're lost."

"Whats your name?" asked the policeman. "Boo," whispered Boo softly.

"What? Speak up, young bear!" the policeman demanded.

"Boo," muttered Boo, this time a bit louder.

"What? What? I can't hear you!" thundered the policeman.

"BOO!" said Boo loudly. So loudly that everyone around him jumped three feet sideways into the air (which is kind of a difficult thing if you think about it).

The policeman jumped so high his helmet came down over his eyes when he landed.

"What…what…" he spluttered, trying to regain his composure. "That's it, young man. It's the police station for you!"

The next thing they knew, the three of them were locked up. Bewildered, (or in Boo's case, bear-wildered), they sat in their small jail cell, till Mr Perera, always the resourceful one, decided that he would demand to see a judge.

After much grumbling, the police took them to court where the judge, a very old man sat up on a High Chair and looked down at them through his glasses.

"Yes. What is the nature of the complaint?" he cried, amiably enough (for he had just finished an afternoon nap). The policeman harrumphed and snorted his way through his statement, claiming that Boo had scared everyone.

"This bear?" inquired the judge, gazing at Boo over his horn-rimmed glasses, "but he seems so friendly."

"Please, sir," whispered Boo, raising his paw. "May I explain?" The kindly judge beckoned him closer to the bench and Boo whispered in his ear.

"The problem is, sir — we were looking for the Magic Trees and we got very very lost. So, it's not really our fault."

"Well, all right then," said the Judge, "But what about this charge of scaring the policeman?"

"Well sir, my name is Boo, and whenever I say it loudly people get scared. So if I promise to say it quietly will you let me and my friends go?"

The judge started to chuckle. Then he started to guffaw. Then he started to roar with laughter. So much so that the entire courtroom stood there and watched in amazement.

"Ladies and Gentlemen, this bear's name is Boo and he wouldn't hurt a fly. Let it now be proclaimed that he may say his name as loudly and as proudly as he wants and let no one say any different."

Boo and his friends beamed at the judge, while the policeman went scarlet, then green and finally crimson (which is easy to do if you're a chameleon).

Boo and his friends felt great. They had been sad to be blamed for something they had not done — and glad that they got a chance to explain themselves.

"And for the record, one more time, young sir," said the judge, wiping the tears of laughter streaming from his eyes. "What is your name?"

Boo climbed onto his back paws, took a deep breath and roared as loudly as he could, "MY… NAME ... IS ... BOO!"

THE CLEVER LITTLE MYNAH

Ruveka Attygalle

The seven sisters flew here and there babbling excitedly, as they always do about something or other. But today they had news that really was of interest to all the other animals.

"There are people in the forest," said one.

"We saw them," said another. "They were in one of their travelling machines. They stopped by the water."

"People?" asked Chuti the little deer nervously. "Are they dangerous?"

"People aren't usually dangerous these days. Mostly they like to watch us animals," said Raja the elephant.

"To watch us? What for?"

"Who knows? People are very strange creatures."

"It was different in the old days," said Nandi, the oldest elephant. Nandi was the oldest animal in the forest. She was even older than Wilbur the tortoise — and he was older than he would ever

admit. Nandi was respected by all the animals because she knew so much about the forest, having lived there so long — and an elephant, as you know, never forgets. The young ones loved to listen to her stories of the old days.

"In the old days," said Nandi, "humans were much fiercer. They used to hunt all kinds of animals for pleasure. All the animals were much more afraid of them then than they are now."

"How awful," said little Chuti.

"We saw the people getting down from their travelling machine," said one of the birds, eager to continue with their story. "They were standing on the banks of the river and talking. They do make the funniest noises." The birds giggled.

"My friend the mynah can make funny noises like that," said Rani, the oldest of the seven sisters. The birds giggled some more.

"Long ago, I knew a mynah," said Nandi, "who could speak human just like them. She used to make us laugh and laugh. She could imitate all the different animals too. She was such a clever little mynah. Milly, that was her name. I wonder what became of her."

"I wish I could do that," said Chuti.

"I remember the mynah bird had a friend just like you, little Chuti — a young deer called Spot. It was an unusually close friendship for a mynah and a deer. They would always be together. The mynah bird would entertain Spot for hours with all the different sounds she could make. She was very proud of her cleverness. One morning she had taught herself to imitate the sound of the dogs in the village. She came rushing up to Spotty to show off her new trick. 'Now don't you two go too far away,' said Spotty's mother. She usually never let Spot out of her sight.

"But it was a beautiful morning and Milly and Spot wandered about happily and started chasing streams of golden butterflies that were rushing along on their annual journey to the mountain. When the butterflies had passed by they realized that they had drifted far away from the other deer and were now quite alone. They heard a rustling deep in the grass. There was something there and it was coming closer. They were terrified. At last they saw Kuveni the terrible

leopard sprinting towards them. Spot ran as fast as he could but the leopard was gaining on him.

"Milly bravely flew at the leopard's face and tried to flap at her eyes with her wings. But the leopard merely waved her away with one paw and laughed. 'Silly little bird,' she said. 'Did you think you could fight a leopard?' She smiled as she came within a whisker's length of poor Spot who was becoming too tired to run. 'I'll have a nice breakfast today,' said the leopard with satisfaction.

"Suddenly the leopard heard the harsh voice of a man. Another man's voice answered it. And then another. There was only one thing that Kuveni

the leopard was afraid of, and that was humans. A British hunter had turned her mother into a hearth rug. She heard the metallic click of a gun preparing to fire. She turned around and ran for her life.

"Poor Spot stood alone, out of breath and shaking with fear. He knew he should run from the hunters but he was too tired. Then, he noticed his friend Milly flying up to him laughing. 'That showed that big fat cat who can fight a leopard,' she said.

"'Was that you?' asked Spot, amazed. He started to laugh. His clever little friend had imitated hunters and frightened off Kuveni, the great leopard.

"'Dear mynah bird, you saved my life,' he said, 'You really are the cleverest bird that ever was.'"

"That was a lovely story," said Chuti.

All the listeners agreed.

"Tell us another one," begged Chuti.

"Another day, my dear little deer, another day," said Nandi and ambled off to her breakfast.

UGLY THE ELEPHANT

Samia Cader

A herd of elephants lived in a temple in Kandy and were looked after by a community of monks. They were a magnificent healthy group of elephants except for one. His skin was splotchy, wrinkly and rough, and he was very thin. The only good thing about him was that he had a magnificent pair of tusks. All the other elephants called him 'Ugly'. They teased him and did not like to play with him. "You are so ugly, we do not want you near us," they said cruelly. The others always seemed to have fun, they worked together in the forest carrying logs, they shared their food and bathed together in the river nearby splashing each other with trunks full of water. But they never included poor Ugly.

Every year, the elephants were taken for the perahara and they wore the most beautiful costumes. But Ugly was never chosen and he was very sad. He did not have any friends, except for a little baby elephant called Lakshmi. She was extremely friendly and playful; a happy little elephant who loved everyone. She enjoyed bath time best — splashing around by the water with the others in the river.

Now, though this elephant was ugly, he was very kind, brave and loved to help others. But it didn't matter — the others still ignored him, called him names, and laughed at him. Every morning when the elephants went to the river they would all have great fun together except for Ugly, who was by himself away from the rest of the herd. They chased him away whenever he approached them, and with tears in his eyes, Ugly would walk away sadly.

One day when the elephants were bathing in the river, baby Lakshmi wandered off by herself searching for leaves and branches that had fallen into the water. She did not realise it, but she had wandered off to the deepest part of the river all alone, where the current was strongest.

Before she realised it, she was carried downstream. She desperately tried to gain a footing on the huge rocks, but could not. Suddenly, her feet slipped and she tumbled into the rising current knocking her head on a rock. Ugly, seeing a movement in the water, rushed over to see what it was, and when he realized it was baby Lakshmi, he shouted, "Hold on, I'm coming!" He ran into the deep water—despite the currents—and dragged her ashore trumpeting loudly. The others in the herd, upon hearing the commotion, came rushing to see what had happened.

"Look," shouted one of the elephants, "it's baby Lakshmi, she is hurt."

They ran towards Lakshmi and saw that she was badly injured, with cuts across her leg and a bruise on her head. They were horrified. The mahouts who were in charge of the elephants rushed over and helped Lakshmi get back on her feet.

A few days later, Lakshmi had recovered and was as cheerful as ever. The others in the herd came and thanked Ugly.

"Thank you so much for what you did, if not for you poor baby Lakshmi may have died," her mother wailed.

"We are so ashamed that we treated you so badly all these years," said Aunty Sita.

"Please forgive us and we would like to be friends with you," said Cousin Nilmini.

"We will never bully or tease you again, we have behaved terribly," said niece Dilani.

"We will never be mean to you again, you are a very kind elephant and we should never have mistreated you all these years," they exclaimed all together.

The chief monk, who witnessed the incident, bought a gift for Ugly. It was a beautiful costume in red and gold for the perahara. In addition to this, Ugly was given an award for bravery for saving Lakshmi's life. Ugly was very happy but he looked at the costume sadly and shook his head.

"How can I wear this costume, I am so ugly, I do not deserve it." The other elephants who had laughed and teased him felt ashamed of themselves. They said, "Please do not worry, we will help make you look beautiful." They applied ointments made out of leaves, herbs and barks of trees and gave him lots of fruit to eat. They scrubbed him down with natural herbs and very soon his skin was no longer splotchy and wrinkly. He began to put on weight and his skin glistened. He began to look magnificent.

When next year's perahara came around, Ugly was the first to be chosen.

"Thank you so much for helping me look splendid. I will never forget what you all have done for me," he told the other elephants. He wore his red and gold velvet costume, and the chief monk from the temple sprinkled gold dust all over his tusks. The others gasped when they spotted him.

"You look so majestic, we cannot believe that you are the same elephant you were before. You have changed beyond recognition." He smiled happily and thanked everyone. Little Lakshmi, wearing a bright pink and silver costume, refused to leave his side.

At last, the time of the perahara dawned. There were thousands of people lined up along the street. There were over two hundred elephants. Photographers were busy taking pictures of the

elephants parading up and down the street. Ugly loved all the excitement; the beautifully decorated elephants, the drummers and glittering dancers in their colourful costumes, the fire eaters, the devil masks, and the carnival-like atmosphere. The people gasped upon seeing Ugly. "Look at his beautiful tusks and the magnificent costume, doesn't he look wonderful," they said. It was the happiest day of Ugly's life. His name was changed to Raja the majestic tusker and each year, he headed the fabulous perahara. He was never known as Ugly ever again.

DULIKA'S GREAT DAY

Kanthi Goonawardane

All the students stood up from their seats when the class teacher, Mrs Perera, came into the class room.

"Good morning, children."

"Good morning, teacher."

"Now sit down all of you. I have an announcement to make." She took a sheet of paper and looked around the class. All the students were gazing at the teacher impatiently waiting to find out the contents of the paper.

"Today is one of my happiest days. Two of you have managed to get grade prizes for a number of subjects."

At once there were murmurs from all parts of the classroom.

"I wonder who?"

"One is surely Dulika."

"Undoubtedly. But, who is the other?"

"Is it Rajitha, or Malinthi, or even me?"

Dulika's heart skipped a beat. She looked longingly at the teacher. Then came the teacher's voice. "Well, children, I won't keep you in suspense any longer. The grade prize for English goes to Malinthi." There were cheers and clapping all round.

"Thank you teacher, I was hoping and praying for it, but I was too afraid to really expect it," said Malinthi, grinning broadly.

"Anyway, now that you got it, try to work harder and get the grade prize next year also," said the teacher, looking encouragingly at Malinthi.

"Yes teacher, I'll try my best," was Malinthi's modest reply.

"Now for the other prizes," the teacher continued, "Grade prizes for Science, Social Science, Health Science, Maths, Religion, and Sinhala go to none other than Dulika."

Deafening applause and cheers made even the teachers from the adjoining classes peep in.

All the girls ran to Dulika to congratulate her.

Dulika was beaming! After a few minutes, the teacher managed to calm the students down and continued, "The prize giving is on the twentieth of this month. Only eighteen days more. The two of you will have to get your clothes etc. ready. You must come in a clean uniform, wearing the school tie, clean white shoes and white socks."

Dulika's smile vanished. She looked down. The teacher noticed this, but did not make any comment. During the interval, the teacher asked Malinthi to join her. They spoke for quite some time.

When Dulika went home that day and shared her news about winning six of the prizes, her parents were elated, but when she mentioned the clean white uniform and the white shoes, they too stopped smiling. She had only two uniforms, and one of them, they reasoned, could be washed and re-washed and bleached to make it white, but what about the shoes and socks? The only pair of shoes she possessed was so worn out that it failed to indicate its original colour.

"Don't worry Putha, I have a little money saved from which I can buy you a pair of cheap socks. We'll see what can be done about the shoes. I'll try to get a loan for that," was her father's consoling reply.

From that day, Dulika's mother started carefully washing one uniform. But no amount of washing or bleaching could give it a bright new colour, though it looked a lot better than it did before. The next day her father brought a pair of socks, the best he could buy for the little money he had. The shoes remained a remote dream.

Days passed by, and Malinthi looked more and more excited but Dulika did not seem to be so enthusiastic. In fact, she looked rather depressed, No classes were held on the ninteenth. The entire day was spent decorating the school hall and premises in preparation for the grand event. Everybody was busy lending a hand. Dulika looked sad, even though she too helped a lot in the work.

During the last period of the day, the class teacher sent for Dulika, and asked her if she was prepared for the following day. Tears started pouring down Dulika's cheeks.

"Don't cry, Dulika. Tell me what's wrong," said the teacher kindly.

"I won't be able to come tomorrow, teacher," stammered Dulika.

"Why?" she asked with concern.

"I don't have white shoes, or a good uniform."

The teacher then reached behind her and handed Dulika a parcel saying, "What you need is here. Wear these and come tomorrow. After the prize giving, I will explain."

Dulika couldn't believe her ears! Was she dreaming, she wondered. She pinched herself and rubbed her eyes. Oh yes! It was real. The parcel was there, and the teacher was looking at her, kindly. Dulika was thrilled. She felt like hugging the teacher, but respect held her back.

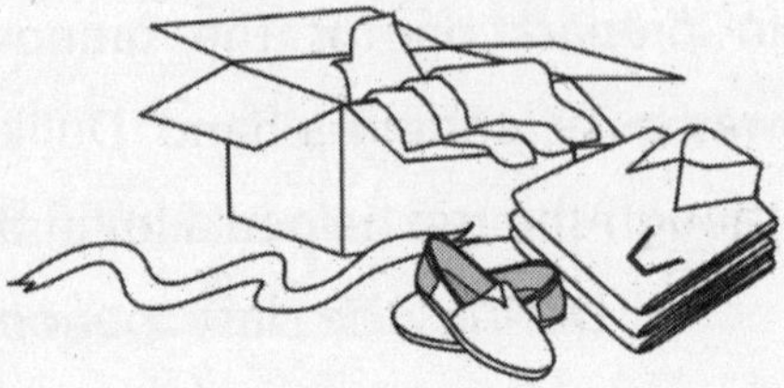

Instead, she fell at the teacher's feet.

"Thank you, oh thank you, teacher. You are an angel!" was all she could whisper.

The last bell rang, and away Dulika went, dancing all the way home.

"Amma, Thaththa, see what I got from school!"

All three of them were thrilled.

The next day at the prize giving, Dulika was the focus of all eyes. Malinthi was the one who admired Dulika the most. Immediately after the grand event, Dulika ran to her teacher and waited for the explanation. Mrs. Perera took her to a lady in a very elegant sari.

"Well, Dulika, this is the lady who gave you the clothes. She is Malinthi's mother."

"Thank you, lady," Dulika said gratefully. "If not for you and my teacher, I wouldn't have been able to be here today."

With that, she fell at the feet of Malinthi's mother, and thanked her.

All those around could see Malinthi and her mother, along with Dulika and her parents, wiping tears of joy.

DRIPPY

Nisreen Jafferjee

This is the story of a little drop of water called Drippy who lived in the great big ocean between the East and the West of our world. Drippy lived a happy and wondrous life with his many, many friends — the thousands of other drops of water that lived beside him. They jostled and bumped along together, travelling to far flung shorelines that edged the vast sea.

There was never a dull moment in the great big ocean. Sometimes Drippy would sink to the bottom of the sea where it was dark and cold. Huge

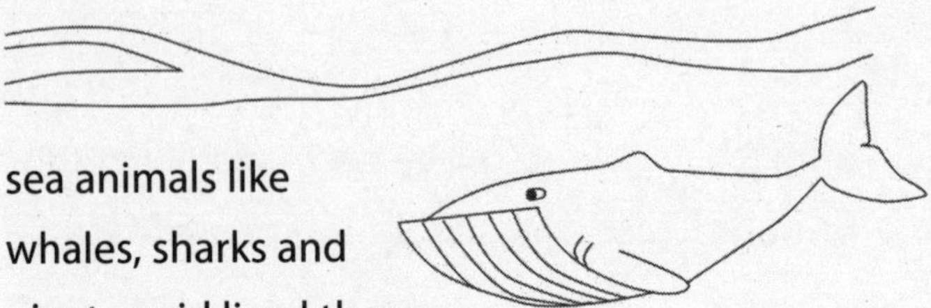

sea animals like whales, sharks and giant squid lived there.

Drippy was wary of these beasts of the deep. He watched with amazement as bigger fish hunted down smaller fish, and was always delighted when the little fish used a clever disguise or quick retreat to escape the bigger fish. Some fish shone brightly to scare off predators, others used their smaller size and speed to get away, and there were still others who pretended to be part of the sea bed.

Drippy, however, was happiest near the surface of the ocean. Here it was bright, warm, and colourful. Massive schools of fish whirled around in frenzied circles like silver underwater tornadoes, making him feel quite dizzy. Endless coral gardens teeming with vibrant fish created fabulous playgrounds. Drippy would spend hours there playing hide and seek with his friends. And when he really wanted excitement and adventure, his favourite place was right at the surface of the ocean.

Drippy loved riding the huge swells in the sea. It was like being swept up a mountain and then sent plunging back down. The biggest thrill for him, though, was near the shoreline where waves sent him crashing onto shore and then yanked him back in to the sea.

"Wheee," cried Drippy, "let's do this again!" The waves crashed onto the beach sending out sprays of water. Drippy would catch these sprays and go flying into the air. He would then tumble back into the sea with a splash. He loved that moment of flying — of feeling weightless, and looking down at everything beneath.

Often, Drippy would lie back in the sea and look up at the birds in the sky. He wished that he could fly as well. The other drops of water in the ocean said that the clouds which floated above the earth contained millions of water drops.

"If you prayed to the Sun God with all your heart, he will help you fly up to the sky, and there you can join the clouds," they said.

"Is that really true?" cried Drippy, "well then I am going to pray to the Sun God every single day. I want to fly. I want to see what the ships look like from above. I want to see what the world looks like beyond this ocean. I want to look over the cliffs and trees that line the beaches we've seen."

Each day when the Sun God rose from the edge of the ocean, Drippy prayed to him.

"Oh Sun God, please grant me my wish. Please help me fly," pleaded Drippy. For several weeks, he prayed continuously from sunrise to sunset till one day the Sun God decided to grant him his wish.

One hot, sunny afternoon, Drippy was lazing around with his friends on the surface of the sea lost in his daily prayer. The Sun God shone brilliantly down till all the drops of water began to sparkle like diamonds. Drippy grew very, very hot. As he got hotter, he began to expand and get lighter. In fact, soon he could barely recognise himself. He was now more like a thin vapour. Slowly, he felt himself rising above the sea.

"I don't believe it," he thought, "I am finally flying!"

Drippy trembled as he rose further up towards the sky. When he looked down he was frightened to be so high up and alone. He looked around and saw big groups of water drops huddled together.

"So it really is true—the clouds are made of millions of drops of water like me," he thought. He slowly manoeuvred further up and attached himself to an enormous cloud. Now in the company of the other drops of water in the cloud, he felt comforted and began to enjoy the feeling of floating in the sky.

He was struck by how large the world was. It was not flat as he had imagined it to be. It was round — a big giant ball covered mostly by water with large chunks of land in between. Sometimes his cloud came down, closer to the earth. Then Drippy could see forests, mountains, great grassy plains, and deserts. He noticed that water was one of the most important reasons for life on earth. Every living thing needed water to stay alive. In fact, most life on earth was near a water source — rivers, lakes, springs and wells. Animals and people used water for various reasons — drinking, cooking, bathing, keeping cool and more. It was terrible, though, to see that a lot of water was being wasted. In some places people had made the lakes and rivers dirty and foul. Drippy was sad because he knew that the polluted water would now cause harm rather than help the creatures on earth. He also saw that where there was no water source, the land was barren. It would be either extremely hot or very very cold. Few plants grew there, and animals and people found it difficult to live in these places.

Drippy saw the great glaciers and large lakes that fed rivers and streams. These rivers and streams snaked across the lands and emptied into the sea. He now realised what an important role he played in keeping the earth alive. He understood that he was part of an incredible water cycle. When water drops like him grew hot, they expanded and became vapours. They then rose from the seas, rivers and lakes towards the sky where they joined to form clouds. Soon, the clouds grew thick with millions of water droplets. When the weather turned cold, the water droplets came together to form bigger and heavier water drops. Then, the earth pulled these bigger drops toward it, where they once again entered the rivers, lakes, and seas. Some rain drops fell on the land and nourished the plants and trees in the forests and fields. These plants and trees provided food and shelter to other living beings.

Drippy puffed with pride at his new sense of importance.

"I am needed on earth," he said to himself. "I do hope that when I go to earth I am respected and used well. If I am wasted, I will no more be a part of this amazing water cycle, and I will not be able to contribute to life on earth. I hope all living things realise that every little drop of water is important. If it is wasted, the earth will be a little less livable." With that thought Drippy turned to the Sun God and prayed that he return to earth again.

The Sun God was happy that Drippy had now learnt the secret to life on earth.

"Go safely and do well by all living things," he said as he blessed Drippy. Then the Sun God dimmed his rays. Cold winds blew towards the clouds. As it got colder, the water droplets held on to each other forming bigger drops. Drippy got very frightened and held onto his companions tightly as well. His cloud was now dark and heavy. Lightning streaked the sky and thunder boomed over the earth. Drippy was terrified as the great cloud shuddered and shook. Suddenly he felt himself being stretched as the earth began to pull him towards it. He tried to hold on tighter but the pull was too strong and soon he found himself falling from the cloud. "Heeeeeelp," screamed Drippy as he moved faster and faster,

speeding down towards the earth. He must have fainted because he didn't remember anything of the fall after that.

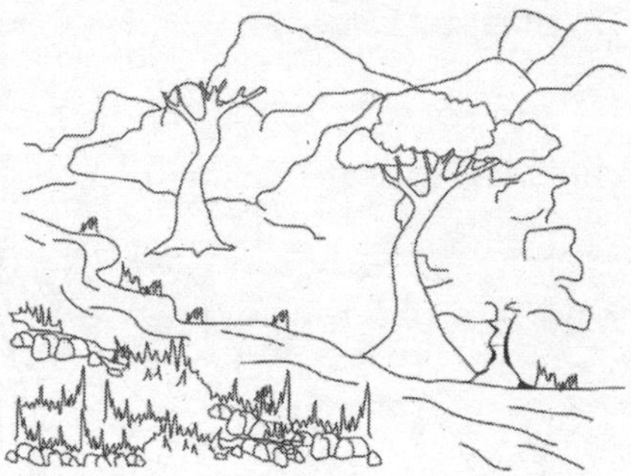

When he woke up, he was sure the events of the night before must have been a terrible dream. As, Drippy found himself bobbing along in a gently flowing stream nestled high up in the mountains. It was a bright and cool morning, and the stream was fresh and clear. He had a blissful day watching the beautiful landscape unravel before him.

Drippy had been on a long and exciting adventure, and learnt so much about the world. But now, he began to miss his home and his friends in the great ocean with all its marvellous creatures. He had learnt that every river eventually leads to the sea.

"I'm going back," he said aloud happily, and readied himself for his journey to the great big ocean.

HITLER THE CAT

Manoshi de Silva

When Hitler was brought to our house by my older brother, he was a proud and arrogant little Persian kitten. The moment he set foot inside he walked around the house like he owned the place. But I must admit, with his striped, thick ginger coat and fury feather-duster like erect tail, he did look quite adorable. He was getting spoilt by the second with all the attention he received and made us all feel like we were in his home, and not the other way around.

The name 'Hitler' came about after he made sure that everyone at home danced to his tune. He'd wake up early in the morning and meow till someone woke up and poured him some milk. Then he'd just play around with anything he'd fancy — my mother's yarn, grandmother's comb, shoes and shoe-laces that belonged to my father and brother or anything else he'd see lying around.

When it came to sleeping, it was pretty much the same. He'd sleep on freshly ironed clothes, on folded clean clothes in the cupboards (when the doors were open,) or even on someone's bed, till he was chased off. He wanted everything his way and was a little dictator. This is what made my sister, who always had her head bent over a history book, name him Hitler. Although we found it funny at the beginning, soon we all started to call him that and couldn't think of a more suitable name for him.

Even though Hitler was proud and moody, when he was in a good mood he'd come and rub against us with his 'purring machine' on full volume. He loved it when I scratched under his chin. He was more attached to me, probably because no one else petted him as much as I did. I often carried him about and held him close to my face, earning a scolding from my grandmother and mother, who worried that fur can cause asthma. But it was a treat for us to watch his antics and he made us laugh doing all sorts of silly things every single day.

Hitler made friends with the village fisherman in no time. He knew the exact time of the fisherman's arrival every morning and would jump on our wall, staring eagerly at the road. When he heard the fisherman's cry, he'd quickly jump down and run forward greeting him with a loud meow. He'd rub around the fisherman's legs continuously crying, while the fisherman weighed and cut the fish, and then threw some odd pieces at Hitler. There was no competition for lucky Hitler because he was the only cat down our lane.

As Hitler grew up, he started dominating our garden as well. All the squirrels and birds that lived in our garden claiming ownership to the ripe fruits were forced to leave. He tried to chase off the butterflies and other little insects. After running all living animals out of our garden, he would roll on the ground and sunbathe in the mornings with his legs in the air. This naughty little fur-ball even banished the cockroaches and lizards from our kitchen and won the hearts of the women folk who worked in the kitchen.

A few months passed; Hitler was now no longer a kitten. He became lazy as he grew up and more moody. Sometimes when I called him, he'd ignore me and groom himself, licking his paw and washing his face. If I tried to pet him, he'd give me a displeased look and cuddle on the stack of old papers, which was also his day-time bed. He responded to his name very promptly only three times a day. That was for breakfast, lunch and dinner.

As his lifestyle became more and more sedentary, he gained weight and became chubby. At times it was difficult to carry him because he was so heavy. The birds and the squirrels occupied our garden once again because they knew the chubby cat in the house couldn't run as fast as he used to. Even if a cockroach approached his face, he pretended not to see it and continued to sleep.

One morning we were woken up with my sister's scream. She was in our grandmother's room kneeling beside the bed and staring as though she had seen a ghost. "I was looking for an old pair of slippers under the bed and look at what I found?" she stuttered. In a cardboard box containing some old clothes, was Hitler — not alone — but with four little suckling kittens! Only then did we realize that our Hitler was a 'she'. It was a funny thing but also a nice surprise. We wondered if we should re-name her but decided against it, continuing to call her Hitler, because that's exactly what she was.

A couple of weeks later, the kittens opened their eyes and started to run about the house. Every minute something crashed or toppled. The

four naughty little fur-balls were wrecking the house, playing silly games. But they were a sight for sore eyes and rarely did anyone blame them or get cross with them, although they were up to such mischief. We knew we'd have them only until they were big enough to be given away to new owners.

Poor Hitler didn't have the energy to do anything else after grooming her kittens and putting up with all their nonsense. The kittens were jumping at her tail, nibbling her ears and harassing her in every possible way. I smiled to myself when I realized that Hitler had competition. There were four little Hitlers in the house and they were in control now.

RUMBLE IN THE JUNGLE

Anthea Senaratna

Lunga the leopard woke up with a start. He had suddenly remembered that today was his turn to preside over the meeting of the Jungle Drama Club.

It was still dark as the sun had not yet shown its bright smiley face on this part of the planet. Lunga gazed at the trees and the leaves flickering in the wind and gave a big wide yawn. He was up during the night hunting for food and right now he felt like having a nice long nap. But this wouldn't be possible — not at the moment anyway, for today was going to be another day for acting and drama for the human visitors to the game park.

Lunga sighed a growly sigh when he thought of the performance he had to put on when the humans — the Horrors, he called them — came to watch him! First he had to stalk, then he had to look fierce, not that he wasn't but he had to wear the look; baring his prominent incisors by opening his mouth really wide so they could have a good look and say, "Oh my gawsh did you see that — what teeth — I managed to get a good shot of it on my iPhone."

Well, time to go. The drama group had gathered deep inside the forest to discuss the proceedings for the day.

Binga the bear had flopped by a tree with his mate and they looked like two humungous lumps of tar! Crocky the croc had come with his buddy and they were sitting there like two ragged rocks!

Peacocks and peahens were in one corner strutting around and muttering something quite incoherent. Now what was the word for a whole crowd of peacocks? Lunga checked the internet, yes, he too had a connection, not only the Horrors! And there it was. Ah! Yes, it could either be a 'muster' of peacocks or an 'ostentation' of peacocks or a 'pride' of peacocks (the lions would definitely object to this last one so thank goodness there were no lions in this jungle!)

The jumbos took up a huge amount of space but then what could they do? They stood tall and huge with gigantic bodies; they flapped their large ears and curled their long trunks and whisked their short tails this way and that. Can you believe that their trunks are really elongated noses, a picking-up device, and a water sprayer? Wow!

A herd of buffalos were looking mournful in another corner. Didn't these guys know how to smile? They wore their horns like crowns on their heads. Dangerous things those were and could pierce right into you if you got too close.

The spotted deer stood at a distance, still and silent, gazing dolefully with their large eyes.

The monkeys were, as usual, making a huge rumpus up on the trees. They were screeching and leaping from branch to branch, hanging by their tails and moving with great agility.

Lunga gave them one big growl, "Shush you idiots. How can I do anything with all of you squawking like that?"

A sounder of fat wild boar, their short tails twitching, trotted along the road — the baby boars ran close to their mothers who nudged them into line. They took care not to get too close to the tree on which Lunga was perched, because they knew that if they roused his temper it could lead to a major confrontation.

Lunga took his seat on the branch of a tree and began to speak in Animal Lingo.

"Oh, my fellow creatures, we have gathered here to discuss the plan for the day. First, we will point out the locations where we will have to be present. Next, we will appoint the participants, then the times — what time should you be there and for how long and, of course, the entertainment one has to perform for the Homo Sapiens. I do suppose you know that means human beings in English." (Lunga loved using Latin words to impress others).

Lunga went on to explain to the animals who were gathered there, “I will be on the big tree at the turn off to Block Two. Elephants! Jimba, please listen to me, (he was extra polite as he recalled the time Jimba’s father jabbed his father with his tusks during a hostile disagreement), you and your wonderful herd, will gather near the trees of Block One.”

He instructed the deer to roam the jungles and the peacocks to perform their famous dances.

“What about us?” Binga the bear wailed. “‘Nothing for us to do?”

"Oh my gosh! You are very important. Hmm why don't you walk on that rock by the river. First one and then the other and then you can do a small climb on that tree nearby so they can take shots of you."

"Ah! We don't want to be shot! We don't want to be killed!" Binga and his friend clutched each other in fear.

"No, you idiot," Lunga growled. "I meant camera shots. Not gun shots."

"Okay. Yeah, we'll walk and climb and look at them to make them happy!" Binga said, recovering quickly.

A croaky sound came through. Lunga turned towards the two crocodiles looking grumpy.

"Ah, yes," Lunga said, "and Crocky and his friend can bask in the sun. Crocky, you have a nice mouth, open it wide please."

The meeting was over. The animals moved around and went back to their allotted places. They had to do their bit for the day, some in the morning, others in the evening and a few even mid-day. After that, when darkness descended, they could retreat into the jungle and do whatever they wanted.

The first jeeps arrived just before sunrise. These were packed with the keen ones who wanted to catch everything before the mid-day sun made it too hot for the animals to come out into the open.

Soon, several other vehicles drove in with all sorts of people inside. They were of different colours, young people and old, fat and thin. Some of them had binoculars hanging round their necks and some had cameras with enormous lenses stretched out like large tubes slung on their shoulders. The jeeps were filled to capacity and the passengers were peering out, trying to see some animal — any animal! It didn't matter which!

A driver jammed on the brakes and the tracker who sat next to him said in a hushed voice, "There's a leopard on that tree. Can you see?" he pointed and all eyes followed. No, none of them could see the leopard. His spotted body was well camouflaged against the leaves.

Lunga moved so they might see him.

Then, Lunga decided his time up the tree was done. He came down slowly so they could have a good look.

There seemed to be a commotion among the jeeps. The occupants in a jeep down the line of some fifteen vehicles shouted. Yes, shouted in the jungle where one is supposed to keep quiet so as not to disturb the animals but did they really care? Bah!

But Lunga didn't seem worried. He sauntered into the bushes, amidst shouts from the onlookers Serves them right for making a ruckus.

The peacocks were lined up a little further away, all ready to dance. They heard the first jeep crashing towards them. They moved cautiously onto the grass by the roadside, and began their

dance. One step forward, one step back, and run around in a little circle. Ta la la la la! The peahen couldn't do much because the peacock was THE dancer of the two. So she hovered on the side while Mr P was prancing up and down, fanning out his exquisite dark blue and aquamarine intricately patterned tail. More jeeps cluttered the roadway overtaking one another so their passengers could get a better view.

The deer skipped along together in between the bushes. Wild boar trotted together lining the road; they weren't going to give the spotted friskies a better audience! Bolay, a young chubby boar, was so fascinated by the peacock's dance that he too began twisting his body and shaking his shoulders and jerking his head from side to side. He even tried to put his tail up and wave it around. His father rushed up to him and gave him a hard knock on the legs.

"Awww. That hurt!"Bolay cried.

"Stop that at ONCE!" his father screamed. "You are disgracing all of us!"

Then it was interval time for the animals and they meandered through the forest awaiting their turns for the next round of visitors.

Mid- afternoon brought on another batch of tourists. They were enthusiastic and sharp-eyed.

"Bear, bear!" someone shouted. "Ah, and another one!" Binga and his friend ambled along looking slyly at the visitors.

A brightly coloured male jungle fowl, his splendid red comb on his head, and his rather plain looking mate were tripping from place to place in search of food. The eagle, with his great hooked beak, perched on top of a tall tree; below, painted storks and white egrets were taking a slow walk through the water. Parrots, kingfishers, barbets, and many other varieties of birds could be seen flying through the jungle, perching from time to time on the branches of the trees. The forest resounded with their calls.

"Ah, there are two crocodiles," someone yelped, and sure enough, on the banks of the villu, was one large crocodile with his mouth open and another slightly submerged in the water, his eyes bulging.

Mama elephant walked past with her little baby by her side. They picked some leaves from the trees and moved quickly into the forest. A short while later a large male elephant came out. He raised his trunk and gave a resounding trumpet call showing off his massive tusks and sending shivers down the spines of the onlookers.

Quite unexpectedly, Dandy, a young male elephant, dashed up to the vehicles and gazed at the stunned occupants.

I'll show them I can dance, too! he thought as he skipped down the road swinging his body from side to side and sat with a hard PLONK on the

sloping edge, but it was too sandy and he just slid down landing upside down on his back with his legs up in the air.

What shall I do, what shall I do? Dandy panicked. *I know, I'll give a loud trumpet and end the performance*. He had forgotten that his trumpet was still undeveloped and when he did try all he could do was say 'Harrumph!' in a weaky squeaky voice! He struggled to his feet and ran into the jungle, while the onlookers roared with laughter!

It was now past six in the evening. The animals wandered into the cool forest. The day's work was over so now they could do as they pleased. Bolay and his friends practiced their dance steps, tok-tok-tok while the elders lay sprawled, eyes shut, making a gurruffing sound. The cicadas screeched and the frogs serenaded one another.

Lunga felt hungry. He stretched his brawny limbs and padded softly into the night.

KING OF THE BEASTS

Sanjaya Senanayake

Although many dinner topics cause great debate,

There is one in particular that turns mate against mate.

It is a topic discussed at all manner of feasts,

About which worthy animal is "King of the Beasts."

"It should be a bird!" declares fashionable Aunt Heather,

As she gobbles up chicken in her hat full of feathers.

"What a pointless conversation," says Great-Uncle Ryan,

"The King of the Beasts has always been the lion."

But although many people regard the lion as King

It is an animal about whose praises I cannot sing.

Sure, a lion's imposing with the strength of King Kong,
It's on the flag of Sri Lanka (formerly Ceylon).
Yet I will shout at the top of my voice,
That a lion as king is a ludicrous choice!
All the male lion does is sleep, eat and roar,
What a lazy feline, what a dreadful bore!
The boy lions make the girls do all the work, you see
This is most unchivalrous and also not 'PC'.
And a lion's bad breath further takes away its gloss,
It's what happens to carnivores who don't dental floss!

Though the fearsome crocodile might seem a worthy winner,
Can you really have a king who eats his subjects for dinner?
And don't forget the croc is an emotional chap,
Who is prone to temper tantrums and liable to snap.
No, a crocodile is unreliable and insincere,
I'm sure you've all have heard of 'crocodile tears'.

As for flightless birds, they're useless things,
Like fish out of water, and canaries that can't sing.
With the Adelie penguin, I can't be any subtler —
its black and white coat makes it look like a butler!
The ostrich has no backbone and won't take a stand,
So the cowardly bird sticks its head in the sand.
In distant New Zealand lives the long-beaked kiwi,
But you can't have a king whose name rhymes with wee-wee!
As for other flightless birds, they're all rather queer,
Such as the emu, cassowary and South American rhea.

If you're looking for a king that reaches great heights,
Seeing the long-necked giraffe is no greater sight.
But the giraffe is shy and doesn't like crowds,
And it's so very tall with its head in the clouds.
It also has an oddity I know to be true —
A big long tongue that is the colour blue!

However, my friends, it's never too late,
To consider the candidacy of the Order of Primates.
To join the Order of Primates is not easy, you see,
You need an opposable thumb and be related to chimpanzees.
And compared to other animals, thinking is not such a strain,
Because all primates have got much bigger brains.
In fact, scientists are adamant, but others do not agree,
That you and I belong to the primate's family tree.
From what I have said, it seems abundantly clear,
That primates should be king — it's a lay-down mazir!

Yet, once again, I'm going to be a frightful bore,
And tell you about primates' itsy-bitsy flaws.

The gorilla for instance is rude to its guests,
It yells and it swears and it beats on its chest.
And while the baboon is intelligent, it is no 'missing link',
It is impetuous, rowdy and has a bum that is pink.
The chimpanzees who live in the African savannahs,
Are addicted to eating tropical fruits and bananas.

And while these foods may be healthy for your heart,
It is best to wear a gas mask when a chimpanzee f**ts!

Elephants are also known as 'pachyderms',
You well may ask the origin of this most unusual term.
'Pachy' means thick and 'derm' is skin, you see,
But don't ask more 'cause it's all Greek to me.
Although they are fine creatures whose praises I can sing,
Elephants have problems which would stop them being king.
It would surprise you to learn that elephants are vain,
Wasting time at the beauticians instead of trying to reign.
Polish on the tusks and mascara on the eyes,
Manicure the nails and wax those thunder thighs.
And don't insult an elephant's trunk — don't you, don't you dare!
Because an elephant wanting a nose-job is a plastic surgeon's nightmare!

Some people have suggested the African gnu,

Some people are silly, what can you do?

This choice has no credibility, not even an ounce,

For how can you have a king whose name you can't even pronounce?

Is it 'Ganu' or 'Nu' or 'Gano', I can't really fathom,

Why didn't they keep it simple and call the poor chap 'Adam'?

Some of you will make what I think is a blunder

By suggesting a king from Australia Down Under.

There's certainly a variety of marsupials to choose,
Such as platypuses, koalas and bush kangaroos.
A king must be tough — that's a vital attribute,
So, unfortunately, the koala is far too cute.
And those violent kangaroos are definitely not right,
They kick and they punch, they box and they bite.
As for platypuses, what can you say about an egg-laying mammal?
It's like a rhino without a horn or a humpless camel.

Now, here's a choice that many would make —
The sleek and slithery, smooth and super snake.
No one can samba like a mamba to the beat of a rattlesnake's rattle,

And there's no more fearsome sight than two cobras at battle.

But the main problem with snakes, says my friend Keith,

Is that our serpentine friends don't have many teeth.

While their two large fangs inflict a fearsome bite,

The absence of teeth is a comical sight.

To rectify this dilemma, many dentists would venture,

Snakes would be better off with a new pair of dentures.

So now here's the winner, straight from its Arctic lair,

The King of the Beasts is none other than the Polar bear!

A polar bear is brave, majestic and more,

Standing on his feet, there's no taller carnivore.

Although he's omnivorous and will eat any meal,

His favourite dish of the day is a freshly caught seal.

And if you ever want a regal residence, let me give you some advice,

Nothing — and I mean nothing — is finer than a polar palace of ice!

A polar bear is intelligent and a fine athlete,

It swims and it jumps and it's swift on its feet.

But although he likes ballroom dancing (there's no bigger fan!)

It's worth noting that a polar bear can barely bear to can-can.

Yes, a polar bear is a beast whose praises I can sing,

And I'm sure he'd make a worthy king.

So thank you for your attention, my good and learned friend,

But now it's time to say goodbye, and let this story end.

I bid you 'Au revoir' with a nod and a bow,

And say goodbye how Italians say it — 'Arriverderci, Ciao!'

Ameena Hussein is an author and co-founder of the Perera Hussein Publishing House. The first collection of *MilkRice*, edited by her, received rave reviews and was taught in Sri Lankan schools. She has just finished editing another collection of children's stories *The Vampire Umpire and other stories.*

CONTRIBUTORS

Afdhel Aziz grew up in Sri Lanka, and now lives in New York. His favourite children's book writers growing up were Enid Blyton, Dr Seuss, Shel Silverstein, and C.S. Lewis.

Sanjaya Senanayake is a doctor who loves to write stories that make children smile.

Nisreen Jafferjee is a mum of two boys who are blessed with wild imagination. She would make up stories as lunch time bribes to encourage them to eat.

Anthea Senaratna loves to write stories and paint pictures. She enjoys talking to her little animal friends and plants! She lives in Colombo with her husband Simon.

Samia Cader is the author of the series *Forest Friends*, Her stories aim to take kids on a colourful journey and instill moral values that provide a great learning experience.

Manoshi de Silva is someone who refused to grow up and therefore still crazy about children's stories. She scribbles and draws cartoons on almost everything.

Ruveka Attygalla is a dreamer. She likes to draw and write and read and sleep.

Kanthi Goonewardene is a school teacher, and likes writing stories for children that have good values.

Created in 2005, POPSICLE BOOKS is the children's arm of the Perera-Hussein Publishing House. Its mission is to create interesting and original books which children will love, giving them a sense of place while opening windows of learning, diversity and culture.

Mythil's Secret

Paduma meets the Sunbird

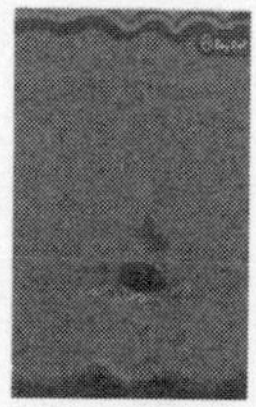

Butterflies Kisses and Turtle Tears

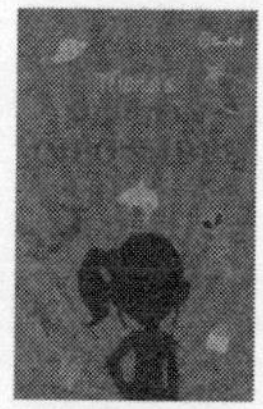

Mona's Mission Impossible

Asiri's Quest

MilkRice

Angel Games and Little Flames

The Vampire Umpire

Three friends and the Big Wave

The Runaway Christmas Tree